Dallas Friday

By Jeff Savage

Lerner Publications Company • Minneapolis

Lerner Publications Company
A division of Lerner Publishing Group
241 First Avenue North
Minneapolis, MN 55401 U.S.A.

Website address: www.lernerbooks.com

Library of Congress Cataloging-in-Publication Data

Savage, Jeff, 1961–
    Dallas Friday / by Jeff Savage.
      p.   cm. — (Amazing athletes)
    Includes bibliographical references and index.
    ISBN-13: 978-0-8225-6595-6 (lib. bdg. : alk. paper)
    ISBN-10: 0-8225-6595-1 (lib. bdg. : alk. paper)
    1. Friday, Dallas, 1986– 1. —Juvenile literature. 2. Wakeboarding—Juvenile literature. I. Title.
GV840.W34F757 2007
797.3'2092—dc22
                                                2006018963

Manufactured in the United States of America
1 2 3 4 5 6 – DP – 12 11 10 09 08 07

TABLE OF CONTENTS

Dallas waits for her run in the women's wakeboarding final at the 2005 Summer X Games.

GOING FOR GOLD

Dallas Friday stood at the start dock with a smile. She gripped the rope handle as the boat in front of her sped away. The rope stretched tight. Dallas went gliding along the water on her wakeboard.

Thousands of fans filled Long Beach Marine Stadium in Southern California. They were there to see Dallas and seven other riders compete in the 2005 Summer X Games wakeboarding finals. The boarder who performed the most daring and creative routine would win the gold medal. Dallas was the favorite. She had won Summer X Games gold medals three of the last four years. And she was still just 18 years old!

Dallas catches some air during her performance at the 2005 Summer X Games.

Dallas carved through the water on the edge of her board. The boat picked up speed. It created a big **wake** behind it. She hit the wake and shot high into the air. Twenty feet above the water, she passed the handle from her right hand to her left. Dallas leaned forward. She looked like a missile flying through the air. Then she lifted her legs so that her board was above her. Raising her right arm up high, Dallas spotted her landing and came down smoothly. The crowd roared. Dallas had just pulled off a perfect other-hand hoochie!

Wakeboarding is similar to waterskiing. Instead of skis, wakeboarders ride on a single board.

Dallas is just five feet two inches tall and weighs 115 pounds. But her small frame is

Dallas reaches back to perform an other-hand hoochie at the Summer X Games.

packed with muscles. She can launch higher than anyone else. "I like going big," Dallas said. "Plus I can do a couple of tricks that no other girls can do. I train hard. I don't like to lose."

Dallas did more tricks out on the **flats** where the water is calm. She tried a batwing for her final move. She leaned back in the air and spun over. She was sailing through the air face down. Her feet were leading the way, and her toes were pointed downward. The she reached between her legs and grabbed her board. The fans cheered again when she landed safely. Dallas had just won the gold medal!

The Friday family—*(from left)*, Robin Sr., Robin Jr., Darla, Dallas, and Chad—pose for a picture.

LEARNING THE ROPES

Dallas Jacqueline Friday was born September 6, 1986, in Orlando, Florida.

Her father worked as a marine biologist. Her mother was a realtor. Dallas has two older brothers named Chad and Robin.

Many people think Dallas was named after the city in Texas. She wasn't. Dallas Friday's father grew up in the small town of Dallas, North Carolina. He named his daughter after that town.

Dallas joined a gymnastics club at the age of eight. "My parents put me in it because I was always jumping around, climbing on walls and stuff like that," said Dallas. Coach Jeff Woods taught Dallas how to perform tricks on the **balance beam** and **uneven bars**. Dallas's favorite event was the **floor exercise**, where she could run and jump across the floor. "I was a natural, I guess you could say, so I started competing," said Dallas. She became the Southeast regional floor champion. Dallas also won a silver medal in the state **all-around** competition.

Dallas started competing in gymnastics competitions when she was eight years old.

Training was difficult. She got plenty of bumps and bruises on the gym floor. "The falls were even hard with mats," she said. "I hit my teeth on the bars, landed on my neck doing a double backflip. A lot of crazy stuff." Dallas practiced each day after school from three until nine. Then she did her homework and fell into bed.

Dallas started wakeboarding when she was 12 years old.

By the age of 12, Dallas was ready to switch sports. She thought about swimming and diving. Her brother Robin suggested wakeboarding. "That's not even a sport!" Dallas said. Robin said that wakeboarding contests were becoming popular. He took Dallas out on a boat and showed her the basics. "I caught on pretty fast," said Dallas. "I was hooked."

Dallas switched from gymnastics to wakeboarding before her 13th birthday. She started by keeping her board on the water and learning **surface tricks**. She figured out how to **body slide** and **grind** the wake. Then she started doing **wake-to-wake** jumps. Soon, Dallas was doing cool tricks in the air.

Wakeboarding uses many of the same skills as gymnastics. "Gymnastics helped me a lot with strength and flexibility," Dallas said.

Dallas stays on the surface of the water as she learns how to wakeboard.

Dallas practices a jump on her wakeboard.

LAUNCHING A CAREER

Dallas was determined to be a wakeboard star. Her mother, Darla, wanted to give her daughter the chance. But Dallas had a lot to learn. She needed a good coach. Dallas and her mom drove to the Orlando Watersports Complex to talk to the world's best wakeboard coach, Mike

Ferraro. The coach was already working with Meaghan Major, Emily Copeland, and other talented boarders. He explained that he had no time to take on another wakeboarder.

Dallas's mother persuaded Ferraro to at least watch Dallas ride. The coach finally agreed. He hooked her up to a rope behind his boat. Dallas performed a series of tricks. Coach Ferraro was amazed. He said, "Your daughter is going to be the first female to make a million dollars riding a wakeboard."

Dallas sits with her first wakeboarding coach, Mike Ferraro.

Dallas's parents borrowed money to pay Coach Ferraro's training fee of $200 per hour. When Dallas was not at school, she was thinking about wakeboarding. She even dreamed of tricks. "I dreamed about a **wrap blind 360** and nailed it the next day," she said.

Dallas soars above the water on her wakeboard.

One of Dallas's first contests was the 2000 Summer X Games. At 13, she was the youngest competitor. She shocked the crowd by taking second place. She won a shiny silver medal. Later that year, she captured a gold medal by winning the America's Cup.

Coach Ferraro knew Dallas's gymnastics training was paying off. "She is used to the pain of hard falls and the strain of working hard every single day," said the coach. "All the girls are afraid, but Dallas is the least afraid, and it's because of her previous training."

"A lot of beginners don't know to stand sideways, and they get all twisted trying to pull their body to face forward," says Dallas. "It's much easier once you get the stance down. Just relax and don't tense up."

Dallas was in such great shape that coaches at Boone High School wanted her to play other sports. The track coach convinced her to compete in the **pole vault**. Dallas loved soaring through the air. She also raced in **sprints**. But her favorite sport was wakeboarding. Her love for the sport was about to pay off.

Dallas shows off a big move.

FORTUNE

A digger is a bad crash on a wakeboard. Dallas has had lots of them. In 2001, she injured her knee. She had surgery to fix it. Before long, she was back on the board and going higher than ever.

Dallas was doing tricks that no one else could match. Some of her favorites were **roll to blind**, **whirlybird**, and **krypt**. Her incredible tricks won her gold medals at the Gravity Games and the Summer X Games.

Dallas's skills and success made her popular with fans. Companies took notice. They offered her thousands of dollars to sponsor their products. Deals with O'Brien wakeboards, Fox

Dallas *(second from left)* poses with fans after winning the gold medal at the 2001 Summer X Games.

Racing, Malibu boats, Bare Sportswear Corporation, and others made Dallas rich. She was earning more than $200,000 a year by her 16th birthday.

Dallas Friday has a funny nickname. Her friends call her Houston Thursday.

Dallas found a new hobby—shopping! "It's my favorite thing to do," she admits. "I buy crazy stuff sometimes, but I have fun with it." Dallas bought fun things such as a snow cone machine and a fog machine. She celebrated getting her driver's license by buying a new car. When she turned 18, she bought two homes on private lakes. She rented one out and moved into the other. For her 18th birthday party at her new house, she had a **halfpipe** built in the backyard so her friends could skate.

When Dallas wasn't playing, she was competing. In 2002, she had to overcome another digger. This time, Dallas broke her back! But after surgery and **physical therapy**, she was back on her board. "I got right back in the water and pushed even harder," she said. "I did not let it hold me back."

Dallas finished second at the Summer X Games that year. She was named Florida's Fittest Female by *Florida Sports Magazine*. In 2003, she won every event she entered except one. She won gold medals at the Summer X Games, Gravity Games, and Vans Triple Crown.

Her most impressive victory came at an event in Portland, Oregon. Her first trick was a whirlybird. She landed awkwardly and felt pain surge through her leg. Dallas climbed into the boat and pulled off her boot. She saw that

Dallas *(center)* stands on the podium after receiving her gold medal at the 2003 Summer X Games.

her ankle was "all blown up." It was swollen and badly injured.

Rather than quit, she jumped back into the water. "I'm going to do this!" she said. Ripping through the water in pain, Dallas captured first place. "At the hospital later, they told me I had broken my ankle," she said.

The Kodak Theatre in Hollywood, California, where the 2004 ESPY Awards were held

FAME

Dallas had become one of the most famous teenage athletes in the United States. In 2003, she appeared on the television show *Switched!* In 2004, she appeared in an episode of *Kim Possible*. One of her proudest moments came on July 14, 2004, at the famous Kodak

Theatre in Hollywood, California. Dallas won an ESPY award for Best Female Action Sports Athlete. No wakeboarder had ever won before. Over 10 million fans across the country had voted for Dallas. "I was shocked! I could not believe they called my name," she said. "This is such a huge milestone for the great sport of wakeboarding and especially for us women! It is one of the happiest and most thrilling moments of my life."

Dallas on the red carpet at the 2004 ESPY Awards

From 2003 to 2005, Dallas entered 34
competitions. She won 32 of them. "I can hear
the crowds cheering when I'm riding," she
says. "It pumps me up to do the best I can!"
She won gold at the Summer X Games in 2004
and 2005.

Dallas *(center)* stands with silver medalist
Emily Copeland *(left)* and bronze medalist Tara
Hamilton *(right)* at the 2005 X Games.

Dallas likes to relax when she isn't wakeboarding.

When Dallas isn't riding, she likes to hang out at the beach. She also likes to go to movies with friends. When she's at home, she likes to play with Jodi, her bird, and Otis, her dog. Her pets also include Elliott, her six-foot python snake.

Dallas spends most of her time on the lake behind a boat. "As long as I stay healthy, I could wakeboard for another 10 years," says Dallas. "In this sport, my body takes a beating. But I try not to think about it. I love this sport so much. I want to do this until I can't walk."

Selected Career Highlights

2006   First place, Wakeboard World Cup
First Place, Masters Water Ski and
   Wakeboard Tournament

2005   U.S. National Champion
First place, Summer X Games
First place, Wakeboard World Cup
First place, Pro Wakeboard Tour, Orlando,
   Florida
First place, Pro Wakeboard Tour, Reno, Nevada

2004   U.S. National Champion
First place, Summer X Games
First place, Wakeboard World Cup
First Place, Masters Water Ski and Wakeboard Tournament
First place, Gravity Games, Perth, Australia
First place, Vans Triple Crown
First place, Pro Wakeboard Tour, Orlando, Florida
First place, Malibu Open, Sacramento, California

2003   First place, Summer X Games
First place, Wakeboard World Cup
First place, Masters Water Ski and Wakeboard Tournament
First place, Gravity Games, Cleveland, Ohio
First place, Vans Triple Crown
First place, Pro Wakeboard Tour, Portland, Oregon
First place, Pro Wakeboard Tour, Orlando, Florida
First place, Malibu Open, Sacramento, California

2002   U.S. National Champion
First place, Vans Triple Crown
First place, Pro Wakeboard Tour, Orlando, Florida
Second place, Summer X Games
Third place, Gravity Games, Cleveland, Ohio

Glossary

all-around: a gymnastics event in which athletes compete on the uneven bars, balance beam, vault, and floor exercise

balance beam: a gymnastics event in which the gymnast performs on a beam that is 4 inches wide and 16 feet long

body slide: a trick in which riders lean back and glide on their backs

flats: the area outside of the wake where the water is smooth and flat

floor exercise: a gymnastics event in which the gymnast performs dance steps and tumbling moves to music on a mat

grind: when riders slide on their boards along the wake

halfpipe: a ramp shaped like the letter "U," or half of a pipe, on which skateboarders or BMX bikers perform tricks

krypt: a trick in which riders extend their bodies with the boards above their heads while they turn a half circle (180 degrees)

physical therapy: exercises used to strengthen an injured part of the body

pole vault: a track event in which people use poles to launch their bodies up and over a bar

roll to blind: a trick in which riders lean straight back, rotate upside down, and then land with their backs facing the boat and with the handle behind their backs

routine: a series of spins, loops, and other tricks that are scored by judges

sprints: track events in which runners race short distances to the finish line

start dock: the structure at the edge of the water, usually made of wood, where riders start their ride

surface tricks: tricks performed while the board is on the surface of the water

uneven bars: a gymnastics event in which the gymnast performs on a set of 8-foot-long bars. One bar is 8 feet high. The other bar is about $5\frac{1}{2}$ feet high.

wake: a wave created behind a boat. A wakeboarder jumps off or slides along a wake.

wakeboard: the board a wakeboarder rides. It is about 4 feet long and 16 inches wide.

wake-to-wake: two waves are created behind the boat, one from each side of the boat. Riders jump from one wake to the other.

whirlybird: a trick in which riders spin and flip while keeping the handle above their heads

wrap blind 360: a trick in which riders wrap the rope around their waists. This allows them to twirl in a circle without having to pass the handle.

Further Reading & Websites

Blomquist, Christopher. *Wakeboarding in the X Games*. New York: PowerKids Press, 2003.

Cooperman, Stephanie. *Wakeboarding: Techniques and Tricks*. New York: Rosen Publishing Group, 2003.

Maurer, Tracy. *Wakeboarding*. Vero Beach, FL: Rourke Publishing, 2003.

Dallas's Website
http://www.dallasfriday.com
Dallas's official website, featuring articles, photos, statistics, and other information about Dallas and her sponsors.

Pro Wakeboard Tour
http://www.prowakeboardotour.com
This wakeboard organization's website features the latest news, as well as highlights of wakeboarders.

Wakeboarder.com
http://www.wakeboarder.com
A website that offers trick tips and descriptions, music and videos, and an online store.

World Wakeboard Association
http://www.thewwa.com
This wakeboard organization's website provides fans with stories of recent events, schedules, and statistics.

Index

Photo Acknowledgments

The images in this book are used with the permission of: © Mike Isler/Icon SMI, pp. 4, 7, 26, 29; © Steven Georges/Press-Telegram/CORBIS, p. 5; Courtesy of the Friday Family, pp. 9, 11, 12, 13, 14, 15, 16, 20, 27; © Steven Hahn Photography 2006, p. 19; © Chris Polk/WireImage.com, p. 23; © Lucy Nicholson/AFP/Getty Images, p. 24; © Frazer Harrison/Getty Images, p. 25.

Front cover: © Mike Isler/Icon SMI.